D0502407

The Lady and the Chocolate

for Nikki

ISBN-13: 978-0-7407-7382-2
ISBN-10: 0-7407-7382-8

08 09 10 11 12 SDB 10 9 8 7 6 5 4 3 2 1

www.edwardmonkton.com

www.andrewsmcmeel.com

ATTENTION: SCHOOLS AND BUSINESSES
Andrews McMeel books are available at quantity discounts with
bulk purchase for educational, business, or sales promotional use.
For information, please write to: Special Sales Department,
Andrews McMeel Publishing, LLC, 1130 Walnut Street,
Kansas City, Missouri 64106.

The LADY and the CHOCOLATE

Edward Monkton

**Andrews McMeel
Publishing, LLC**
Kansas City

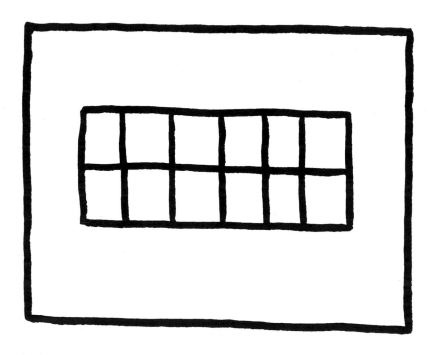

"Hello, Lady," said the Chocolate.

"Hello, Chocolate," said the Lady.

"You want me, Lady, don't you?" said the chocolate. "You want me! You WANT ME!"

"No, Chocolate," said the Lady, "I do not want you for I am STRONG. I can resist my FICKLE urges and my FRIVOLOUS desires."

"But you **NEED** me, Lady," said the Chocolate. "You know you do!"

"No, Chocolate," said the Lady. "I do not need you, for the weight that you put onto my THIGHS, my WAIST and my BOTTOM is not worth the satisfaction of the eating."

"Ah," said the Chocolate, "but think of the rich, SILKY pleasure as I touch your LIPS.

"Think of the dark, velvet SWEETNESS as I melt on your tongue.

"Think of the surge of HAPPINESS as I dissolve inside you and we become ONE!"

"Eat me, Lady, and I will tell no one. Eat me! Eat me!

EAT ME!"

"**NO!**" shouted the Lady. "Stop! You are **CRUEL**! It is true, Chocolate, that in eating you there is great **PLEASURE**. But after the pleasure there is **SICKNESS** and there is **GUILT**.

"I shall not EAT YOU!"

"But, Lady," said the Chocolate, "being **EATEN** is the only reason for my existence."

The Chocolate looked at the Lady with an expression of the utmost sorrow and a single **TEAR** fell to the floor.

"Are you to deny me the REASON for my EXISTENCE?"

Now, the Lady was a lady of great KINDNESS and COMPASSION, as many Ladies are, and she could not help her HEART from going out to the Chocolate.

"No, Chocolate," said the Lady.
"I would not do that."

And, with a touch of infinite
GENTLENESS, the Lady
picked up the Chocolate
and she began to EAT.

And, having eaten the chocolate, the Lady was overcome by feelings of PLEASURE more WONDERFUL than she had ever known before.

And, henceforth, let **ALL** ladies know that it is not **THEY** who need CHOCOLATE for happiness. It is CHOCOLATE that needs **THEM**.

And, in eating, they are performing a very great and **GENEROUS** service indeed.

THE END